INTRODUCTION

OF

THE POWER LOOM,

AND

ORIGIN OF LOWELL.

BY NATHAN APPLETON.

Printed for the Proprietors of the Locks and Canals on Merrimack River.

LOWELL, MASSACHUSETTS:
PRINTED BY B. H. PENHALLOW,
1858.

INTRODUCTION.

June 21, 1858.

Hon. Nathan Appleton: —

Dear Sir,—

It has often occurred to us that there are many facts connected with the history of the City of Lowell, which either are not known to the present generation, or rest upon uncertain and fast perishing tradition; but which may be gathered up and preserved by persons yet living, who bore an important part in laying its foundations; and are personally acquainted with the most, even of the minute details, of those interesting transactions.

That history, so honorable to its founders, is worthy of preservation. It must speak, not merely of the setting up there of factories and spindles, but of the wise and prudent foresight, so characteristic of the New England character; which in the beginning made provision for religious worship, schools, a hospital for the sick, and established a system of management, well calculated to preserve the morals of the people there to be gathered; a large portion of them the young of both sexes, temporarily brought from their homes in the country, and taken from the immediate care and oversight of their parents and friends, as operatives in the mills, under circumstances peculiarly requiring great care and prudence on the part of their employers, to preserve and maintain the high character of the rural population. How liberally these requirements were met, how generous a provision was from the beginning made by those who laid those foundations, no one knows better than yourself.

You, Sir, were engaged from the first, with the gentlemen who turned their attention to the Pawtucket Falls on Merrimack River, as a power eminently fit for large manufacturing operations; and to the present site of Lowell as a proper locality for the use of that power; and for the building of a city, as consequent upon the placing there of those large establishments, which form the principal source of its growth and support. And you acted so prominent a part, in the formation and conduct of the Companies that purchased the land and water-power there, and have continued to the present time, not only your pecuniary interest, but a personal participation in the management of the principal establishments, that you have it in your power to furnish information upon the subject we have mentioned, of great value, not only at the present time, but which will increase with the lapse of years.

We hope, therefore, that you will, in such form as may be most agreeable to you, write out and publish, such things as occur to you as likely to be desirable; and we venture the suggestion, that things which may perhaps seem trifling in themselves, become interesting in such a connection. We trust too, that you will not be restrained in the narration, by the fact that you will often have occasion to speak of yourself, and of your own acts, as otherwise, much of that which is most valuable will be omitted or imperfectly stated.

Should you feel willing to give us, as you are able to do, a more extended view of the rise and progress of the Cotton manufacture in this country, than would necessarily be embraced in the history of Lowell, it would have a still wider interest, and would make known, more generally, the value and importance of the services of some of those distinguished men, who so largely contributed to its successful establishment, with whom you were so intimately associated.

Be assured, that by complying with our request, you will perform a most useful work, and gratify many of your numerous friends and acquaintances, but none more than,

Your Ob'dt Serv'ts,

F. B. CROWNINSHIELD,
Treas. Merrimack Man'g Co.
THOS. G. CARY,
Pres't Prop'rs of Locks & Canals.
JAMES B. FRANCIS,
Agent Prop'rs of Locks & Canals.

BOSTON, SEPT. 1, 1858.

DEAR SIRS:—

I have given particular attention to your interesting communication, on the subject of committing to paper, my reminiscences of particulars connected with the early history of Lowell, and the cotton manufacture.

The idea of doing so has frequently been pressed upon me, and has naturally attracted my attention. My greatest obstacle has been, the necessity which it involves, of using so much the personal pronoun, which would appear more properly in a posthumous autobiography. Your very kind urgency has however, overcome my scruples, connected with the circumstance, that I am now approaching the age of pardonable garrulity, which allows the octogenarian a license to talk of himself. I am, it is true, the survivor of my early associates in this matter. I can claim for myself no other merit, than a cordial co-operation with Messrs. Lowell, Jackson, Boott and others the more active parties in establishing the cotton manufacture, on the principle of making every possible provision for the moral character and respectability of the operatives. I naturally feel a degree of satisfaction, in the part which I have thus performed in the introduction of this manufacture, so important in every point of view to the interest of the whole country. With these views I submit the accompanying manuscript to your disposition, and am very truly

Your very Ob'dt Ser'vt,

NATHAN APPLETON.

Messrs. F. B. CROWNINSHIELD,
THOMAS G. CARY, AND
JAMES B. FRANCIS.

INTRODUCTION OF THE POWER LOOM.

My connection with the Cotton Manufacture takes date from the year 1811, when I met my friend Mr. Francis C. Lowell, at Edinburgh, where he had been passing some time with his family. We had frequent conversations on the subject of the Cotton Manufacture, and he informed me that he had determined, before his return to America, to visit Manchester, for the purpose of obtaining all possible information on the subject, with a view to the introduction of the improved manufacture in the United States. I urged him to do so, and promised him my co-operation. He returned in 1813. He and Mr. Patrick T. Jackson, came to me one day on the Boston exchange, and stated that they had determined to establish a Cotton manufactory, that they had purchased a water power in Waltham, (Bemis's paper mill,) and that they had obtained an act of incorporation, and Mr. Jackson had agreed to give up all other business and take the management of the concern.

The capital authorized by the charter was four hundred thousand dollars, but it was only intended to raise one hundred thousand, until the experiment should be fairly tried. Of this sum Mr. Lowell and Mr. Jackson, with his brothers, subscribed the greater part. They proposed to me that I should take ten thousand of this subscription. I told them, that theoretically I thought the business ought to succeed, but all which I had seen of its practical operation was unfavorable; I however was willing to take five thousand dollars of the stock, in order to see the experiment fairly tried, as I knew it would be under the management of Mr. Jackson; and I should make no complaint under these circumstances, if it proved a total loss. My proposition was agreed to, and this was the commencement of my interest in the cotton manufacture.

On the organization of the Company I was chosen one of the Directors, and by constant communication with Messrs. Lowell and Jackson, was familiar with the progress of the concern.

The first measure was to secure the services of Paul Moody, of Amesbury, whose skill as a mechanic was well known, and whose success fully justified the choice.

The power loom was at this time being introduced in England, but its construction was kept very secret, and after many failures, public opinion was not favorable to its success. Mr. Lowell had obtained all the information which was practicable about it, and was determined to perfect it himself. He was for some months experimenting at a store in Broad street, employing a man to turn a crank. It was not until the new building at Waltham was completed, and other machinery was running, that the first loom was ready for trial. Many little matters were to be overcome or adjusted, before it would work perfectly. Mr. Lowell said to me that he did not wish me to see it until it was complete, of which he would give me notice. At length the time arrived. He invited me to go out with him and see the loom operate. I well recollect the state of admiration and satisfaction with which we sat by the hour, watching the beautiful movement of this new and wonderful machine, destined as it evidently was, to change the character of all textile industry This was in the autumn of 1814.

Mr. Lowell's loom was different in several particulars from the English loom, which was afterwards made public. The principal movement was by a cam, revolving with an eccentric motion, which has since given place to the crank motion, now universally used; some other minor improvements have since been introduced, mostly tending to give it increased speed.

The introduction of the power loom made several other changes necessary in the process of weaving. The first was in the dressing, for which Mr. Horrocks of Stockport, had a patent, and of which Mr. Lowell obtained a drawing. On putting it in operation, an essential improvement was made, by which its efficiency was more than doubled. This Waltham dressing machine continues in use, with little change from that time. The stop motion, for winding on the beams for dressing, was original with this Company.

2

The greatest improvement was in the double speeder. The original fly-frame introduced in England, was without any fixed principle for regulating the changing movements necessary in the process of filling a spool. Mr. Lowell undertook to make the numerous mathematical calculations necessary to give accuracy to these complicated movements, which occupied him constantly for more than a week. Mr. Moody carried them into effect by constructing the machinery in conformity. Several trials at law were made under this patent, involving with other questions, one, whether a mathematical calculation could be the subject of a patent. The last great improvements consisted in a more slack spinning on throstle spindles, and the spinning of filling directly on the cops, without the process of winding. A pleasant anecdote is connected with this last invention. Mr. Shepherd, of Taunton, had a patent for a winding machine, which was considered the best extant. Mr. Lowell was chaffering with him about purchasing the right of using them on a large scale, at some reduction from the price named. Mr. Shepherd refused, saying "you must have them, you cannot do without them, as you know, Mr. Moody." Mr. Moody replied — "I am just thinking that I can spin the cops direct upon the bobbin." "You be hanged," said Mr. Shepherd. "Well, I accept your offer." "No," said Mr. Lowell, "it is too late."

From the first starting of the first power loom, there was no hesitation or doubt about the success of this manufacture. The full capital of four hundred thousand dollars was soon filled up and expended. An addition of two hundred thousand was afterwards made, by the purchase of the place below in Watertown.

After the peace in 1815, I formed a new copartnership with Mr. Benjamin C. Ward. I put in the capital for the purpose of importing British goods, with the understanding that I was not to perform any part of the labor of carrying on the business. I was content with a moderate fortune, but not willing to disconnect myself entirely from business. An accidental circumstance occasioned the continuance of this copartnership until 1830.

At the time when the Waltham Company first began to produce cloth there was but one place in Boston at which domestic goods were sold. This was at a shop in Cornhill kept by Mr. Isaac Bowers, or rather by Mrs. Bowers. As there was at this time only one loom in operation, the quantity accumulating was not very great. However, Mr. Lowell said to me one day that there was one difficulty which he had not apprehended, the goods would not sell. We went together to see Mrs. Bowers. She said every body praised the goods, and no objection was made to the price, but still they made no sales. I told Mr. Lowell, the next time they sent a parcel of the goods to town, to send them to the store of B. C. Ward & Co., and I would see what could be done. The article first made at Waltham, was precisely the article of which a large portion of the manufacture of the country has continued to consist; a heavy sheeting of No. 14 yarn, 37 inches wide, 44 picks to the inch, and weighing something less than three yards to the pound.

That it was so well suited to the public demand, was matter of accident. At that time it was supposed no quantity of cottons could be sold without being bleached; and the idea was to imitate the yard wide goods of India, with which the country was then largely supplied. Mr. Lowell informed me that he would be satisfied with twenty-five cents the yard for the goods, although the nominal price was higher. I soon found a purchaser in Mr. Forsaith, an auctioneer, who sold them at auction at once, at something over thirty cents. We continued to sell them at auction with little variation of the price. This circumstance led to B. C. Ward & Co. becoming permanently the selling agents. In the first instance I found an interesting and agreeable occupation in paying attention to the sales, and made up the first account with a charge of one per cent. commission, not as an adequate mercantile commission, but satisfactory under the circumstances. This rate of commission was continued, and finally became the established rate, under the great increase of the manufacture. Thus, what was at the commencement rather unreasonably low, became when the amount of annual sale, concentrated in single houses amounted to millions of dollars, a desirable and profitable business.

Under the influence of the war of 1812, the manufacture of cotton had greatly increased, especially in Rhode Island, but in a very imperfect manner. The effect of the peace of 1815 was ruinous to these manufacturers.

In 1816 a new tariff was to be made. The Rhode Island manufacturers were clamorous for a very high specific duty. Mr. Lowell was at Washington, for a considerable time, during the session of Congress. His views on the tariff were much more moderate, and he finally brought Mr. Lowndes and Mr. Calhoun, to support the minimum of $6\frac{1}{4}$ cents the square yard, which was carried.

In June I816, Mr. Lowell invited me to accompany him in making a visit to Rhode Island, with a view of seeing the actual state of the manufacture. I was very happy to accept his proposition. At this time the success of the power loom, at Waltham, was no longer matter of speculation or opinion: it was a settled fact. We proceeded to Pawtucket. We called on Mr. Wilkinson, the maker of machinery. He took us into his establishment — a large one; all was silent, not a wheel in motion, not a man to be seen. He informed us that there was not a spindle running in Pawtucket, except a few in Slater's old mill, making yarns. All was dead and still. In reply to questions from Mr. Lowell, he stated, that during the war the profits of manufacturing were so great, that the inquiry never was made whether any improvement could be made in machinery, but how soon it could be turned out. We saw several manufacturers; they were all sad and despairing. Mr. Lowell endeavored to assure them that the introduction of the power loom would put a new face upon the manufacture. They were incredulous;—it might be so, but they were not disposed to believe it. We proceeded to Providence, and returned by way of Taunton. We saw, at the factory of Mr. Shepherd, an attempt to establish a vertical power loom, which did not promise success.

By degrees, the manufacturers woke up to the fact, that the power loom was an instrument which changed the whole character of the manufacture; and that by adopting the other improvements which had been made in machinery, the tariff of 1816 was sufficiently protective.

Mr. Lowell adopted an entirely new arrangement, in order to save labor, in passing from one process to another; and he is unquestionably entitled to the credit of being the first person who arranged all the processes for the conversion of cotton into cloth, within the walls of the same building. It is remarkable how few changes have since been made from the arrangements established by him, in the first mill built at Waltham. It is also remarkable, how accurate were his calculations, as to the expense at which goods could be made. He used to say, that the only circumstance which made him distrust his own calculations, was, that he could bring them to no other result but one which was too favorable to be credible. His calculations, however, did not lead him so far as to imagine that the same goods which were then selling at thirty cents a yard, would ever be sold at six cents, and without a loss to the manufacturer, as has since been done in 1843, when cotton was about five or six cents a pound. His care was especially devoted to arrangements for the moral character of the operatives employed. He died in 1817, at the early age of 42, beloved and respected by all who knew him. He is entitled to the credit of having introduced the new system in the cotton manufacture, under which it has grown up so rapidly. For, although Messrs. Jackson and Moody were men of unsurpassed talent and energy in their way, it was Mr. Lowell who was the informing soul, which gave direction and form to the whole proceeding.

The introduction of the cotton manufacture in this country, on a large scale, was a new idea. What would be its effect on the character of our population was a matter of deep interest. The operatives in the manufacturing cities of Europe, were notoriously of the lowest character, for intelligence and morals. The question therefore arose, and was deeply considered, whether this degradation was the result of the peculiar occupation, or of other and distinct causes. We could not perceive why this peculiar description of labor should vary in its effects upon character from all other occupation.

There was little demand for female labor, as household manufacture was superseded by the improvements in machinery. Here was in New England a fund of labor, well educated and virtuous. It was not perceived how a profitable employment has any tendency to deteriorate the character. The most efficient guards were adopted in establishing boarding houses, at the cost of the Company, under the charge of respectable women, with every provision for religious worship. Under these circumstances, the daughters of respectable farmers were readily induced to come into these mills for a temporary period.

The contrast in the character of our manufacturing population compared with that of Europe, has been the admiration of the most intelligent strangers who have visited us. The effect has been to more than double the wages of that description of labor from what they were before the introduction of this manufacture. This has been, in some measure, counteracted, for the last few years, by the free trade policy of the government; a policy, which fully carried out, will reduce the value of labor with us, to an equality with that of Europe.

The following are the changes in the price of the article first manufactured at Waltham.

1816, - - - -	30 cents per yard.
1819, - - - - -	21 " " "
1826, - - - -	13 " " "
1829, - - - - -	8½ " " "
1843, - - - -	6½ " " "

From that time, the price has fluctuated with the price of cotton, from 7 to 9 cents per yard.

THE ORIGIN OF LOWELL.

The success of the Waltham Company made me desirous of extending my interest in the same direction. I was of opinion, that the time had arrived, when the manufacture and printing of calicoes might be successfully introduced into this country. In this opinion Mr. Jackson coincided, and we set about discovering a suitable water power. At the suggestion of Mr. Charles H. Atherton, of Amherst, N. H., we met him at a fall of the Souhegan river, a few miles from its entrance into the Merrimack, but the power was insufficient for our purpose. This was in September, 1821. In returning, we passed the Nashua river, without being aware of the existence of the fall, which has since been made the source of so much power by the Nashua Company. We only saw a small grist mill standing near the road, in the meadow, with a dam of some six or seven feet.

Soon after our return, I was at Waltham one day, when I was informed that Mr. Moody had lately been at Salisbury, when Mr. Ezra Worthen, his former partner, said to him, "I hear Messrs. Jackson and Appleton are looking out for water power. Why dont they buy up the Pawtucket Canal? That would give them the whole power of the Merrimack, with a fall of over thirty feet." On the strength of this, Mr. Moody had returned to Waltham by that route, and was satisfied of the extent of the power which might be thus obtained, and that Mr. Jackson was making inquiries on the subject. Mr. Jackson soon after called on me, and informed me that he had had a correspondence with Mr. Thomas M. Clark, of Newburyport, the Agent of the Pawtucket Canal Company, and had ascertained that the stock of that Company, and the lands necessary for using the water power, could be purchased at a reasonable rate, and asked me what I thought of taking hold of it. He stated that his engagement at Waltham would not permit him to take the management of a new Company, but he mentioned Mr. Kirk Boott as having expressed a wish to take the management of an active manufacturing concern, and that he had confidence in his possessing the proper talent for it. After a consultation, it was agreed that he should consult Mr. Boott, and that if he would join us we would go on with it. He went at once to see Mr. Boott, and soon returned to inform me that he entered heartily into the project; and we immediately set about making the purchases. Until these were made, it was necessary to confine all knowledge of the project to our own three bosoms. Mr. Clark was employed to purchase the necessary lands, and such shares in the Canal as were within his reach, whilst Mr. Henry Andrews was employed in purchasing up the shares owned in Boston.

I recollect the first interview with Mr. Clark, at which he exhibited a rough sketch of the Canal, and the adjoining lands, with the prices which he had ascertained they could be purchased for. He was directed to go on and complete the purchases, taking the deeds in his own name, in order to prevent the project taking wind prematurely. The purchases were made accordingly, for our joint account, each of us furnishing funds as required by Mr. Boott, who was to keep the accounts.

Our first visit to the spot was in the month of November, 1821, and a slight snow covered the ground. The party consisted of Patrick T. Jackson, Kirk Boott, Warren Dutton, Paul Moody, John W. Boott and myself. We perambulated the grounds, and scanned the capabilities of the place, and the remark was made that some of us might live to see the place contain twenty thousand inhabitants. At that time there were, I think, less than a dozen houses on what now constitutes the city of Lowell, or rather the thickly settled parts of it; — that of Nathan Tyler, near the corner of Merrimack and Bridge streets, that of Josiah Fletcher, near the Boott Mills, the house and store of Phineas Whiting, near Pawtucket Bridge, the house of Mrs. Warren, near what is now Warren street, the house of Judge Livermore, east of Concord river, then called Belvidere, and a few others.

Formal articles of association were drawn up, bearing date the first of December, 1821. They are recorded in the records of the Merrimack Manufacturing Company, as follows: —

" The subscribers hereunto, intending to form an association for the purpose of manufacturing and printing cotton cloth, hereby enter into the following articles of agreement.

" Art. 1. We will petition the Legislature, as soon as may be, for an act of incorporation under the name of The Merrimack Manufacturing Company.

" Art. 2. The capital stock shall be divided into six hundred shares.

" Art. 3. Assessments may be laid on said shares from time to time, as the Company, at any legal meeting, shall direct, and payable at such times as the Company shall appoint. The whole amount of such assessments, however, on each of said shares, shall not exceed one thousand dollars.

Art. 4. Should it hereafter be deemed expedient to increase the capital stock of said Company, it shall be done by the creation of new shares, and the subscribers hereunto, their heirs and assigns, shall be entitled to take one fifth part of the new shares so created for that purpose, to be divided among them, their heirs and assigns, in proportion to the stock now subscribed for; and another one fifth part of the new shares so created, shall be disposed of by the Company in such manner as the majority of them shall direct; but the rights and privileges hereby reserved to the subscribers, their heirs and assigns, shall cease when the capital stock hereinafter subscribed for shall have been doubled. The remaining three-fifths of said new shares shall be divided among those who hold stock at the time of such increase, in proportion to their stock.

" Art. 5. We hereby appoint Kirk Boott, Treasurer and Agent of said Company, for five years from the first day of January, A. D. one thousand eight hundred and twenty-two, and agree that he shall be paid three thousand dollars a year for his services in such capacities.

" Art. 6. Whereas, we have been informed that the Proprietors of the Locks and Canals on Merrimack River, are possessed of valuable mill seats and water privileges; and whereas Kirk Boott has, with our consent, advanced money for the purchase of shares in the stock of that Corporation, and of lands thereto adjoining, we hereby confirm all he has done in the premises, and further authorize him to buy the remainder of the shares in said stock, and any lands adjoining the Locks and Canals he may judge it for our interest to own, and also to bargain with the above named Corporation for all the mill seats and water privileges they may own. He must in all cases be governed by such advice and direction, as he may receive from the Company, or any committee duly appointed by them.

"Art. 7. The shares to be subscribed for by Article 4, are to be paid for at the times and in the manner directed by the Company.

"Art. 8. If any person should refuse or neglect to subscribe for the whole number of shares he is entitled to by Article 4, the shares not so subscribed for, shall belong to the Company, to be disposed of as they may appoint.

"Art. 9. Until an act of incorporation shall have been obtained, and the Company organised under the same, the business shall be conducted as the majority of the associates may direct, at meetings duly notified and held as hereafter provided for.

"Art. 10. The first meeting of the associates shall be notified in writing, by the Agent, to be held on or before the fifteenth of December, one thousand eight hundred and twenty-one, at 4 o'clock, P. M., at the house of P. T. Jackson, Esq., in Winter street.

"Art. 11. At their first meeting, the associates shall appoint a clerk, and determine in what manner all future meetings shall be notified and held.

"Art. 12. At all meetings, each person shall have as many votes as shares, and all matters shall be determined by a majority of the votes given. Any person may vote by proxy, authorised by power of attorney.

"Art. 13. Should it be determined by a majority of the original associates, subscribers hereunto, that it would be for the interest of the whole, to give to any persons shares in the stock, at cost, we each agree to give up the number of shares so required, in proportion to the stock we now subscribe for, provided we receive the amount we shall have paid thereon, with interest.

"Art. 14. Each subscriber agrees to take and pay for the number of shares set against his name in this original subscription, on the terms prescribed in the preceding articles of agreement.

"Boston, December 1st., 1821.

"Kirk Boott, Ninety Shares, - - - - - -	90
"John W. Boott, Ninety Shares, - - - -	90
"N. Appleton, One Hundred and Eighty Shares,	180
"P. T. Jackson, One Hundred and Eighty Shares,	180
"Paul Moody, Sixty Shares, - - - - - -	60
	600

"At a meeting at the house of P. T. Jackson, 7th December, it was voted that the following persons may be permitted to subscribe, in conformity with Article 13.

"Dudley A. Tyng,	5 shares,	Thomas M. Clark,	2 shares,
"Warren Dutton,	10 "	D. Webster,	4 "
"Timothy Wiggin,	25 "	Benj. Gorham,	5 "
"William Appleton,	25 "		
"Eben Appleton,	15 "	Nath'l Bowditch,	4 "

"*Voted*, That N. Appleton be a committee to write T. Wiggin for an answer.

"*Voted*, That we will sell to the Boston Manufacturing Company 150 shares, at 10 per cent. advance; to be supplied by P. T. Jackson 40 shares, N. Appleton 40, Paul Moody 30, J. W. Boott 20, Kirk Boott 20."

An Act of Incorporation was granted 5th February, 1822. The first meeting of Stockholders took place on the 27th February, at which By-Laws were adopted and Directors chosen, as follows: — Warren Dutton, Patrick T. Jackson, Nathan Appleton, William Appleton, Israel Thorndike Jr., John W. Boott; Kirk Boott, Treasurer and Clerk. An assessment was made of 500 dollars per share, to be called for by the Directors. The shares in the Locks and Canals to be conveyed to the several Directors in trust. At a meeting of the

Directors, the same day, Warren Dutton was chosen President. 200 dollars per share was voted to be paid on the 1st. of April. Patrick T. Jackson and Nathan Appleton were appointed a committee to settle Mr. Boott's account, which contained 18,339 dollars for lands of Nathan Tyler, Josiah Fletcher, Joseph Fletcher and Moses Cheever, and 30,217 dollars paid for 339 shares in the Locks and Canals.

The Pawtucket Canal belonged to a Company incorporated in 1792, by the name of "The Proprietors of the Locks and Canals on Merrimack River," apparently established originally with the view of making the Merrimack River navigable to Newburyport. This object was, in a great measure, defeated by the incorporation in 1793 of the Middlesex Canal, opening a direct communication with Boston. A canal, of very moderate dimensions, was, however, made around Pawtucket Falls, for the passage of rafts of wood and lumber. The income, up to 1820, hardly averaged $3\frac{1}{2}$ per cent. per annum, which made the purchase of the stock an easy matter. It consisted of 600 shares, on which 100 dollars had been paid, each.

The enlargement of this canal, and the renewal of the locks, was the first and most important measure to be accomplished by the new Company. It was decided to make it sixty feet wide and eight feet deep, which, it was estimated, would furnish fifty mill powers. This was commenced with the opening Spring of 1822, and prosecuted with the utmost vigor; but it was soon ascertained that it could not be accomplished in the manner proposed, in one season. Its cost was upwards of 120,000 dollars.

It was decided to place the mills of the Merrimack Company where they would use the whole fall of thirty feet. Mr. Moody said he had a fancy for large wheels. In the mean time a new canal was to be made to the Merrimack River, mills were to be built, a house for Mr. Boott, and boarding houses for the operatives. A contract was made with the Boston Manufacturing Company, or Waltham Company, for machinery for two mills. As it was all important to the Merrimack Company to have the use of the patents of the Waltham Company, and especially to secure the services of Mr. Moody, it was finally arranged to equalise the interest of all the stockholders in both companies, by mutual transfers, at rates agreed upon, so that there was no clashing of interest in any case. This could only be done by a strong feeling of mutual interest in favor of the measure, and a liberal spirit of compromise in carrying it out. Under this arrangement, it was agreed, in August 1823, to pay the Waltham Company 75,000 dollars for all their patterns and patent rights, and to release Mr. Moody from his contract in their service.

In December, 1822, Messrs. Jackson and Boott were appointed a committee to build a suitable church; and in April 1824, it was voted that it should be built of stone, not to exceed a cost of nine thousand dollars. This was called St. Anne's church, in which Mr. Boott, being himself an Episcopalian, was desirous of trying the experiment whether that service could be sustained. It was dedicated by Bishop Griswold, but the Directors of the Merrimack Company never intended to divest themselves of the control of it. Liberal grants of land were made for other places of worship, and subscriptions freely made by the stockholders for different religious societies.

The first wheel of the Merrimack Company was set in motion on the first of September, 1823. In 1825 five hundred dollars were appropriated for a Library. Three additional mills were built. In 1829 one mill was burnt down; in 1853 another. In 1825, Mr. Dutton going to Europe, Nathan Appleton was appointed President. The first dividend of one hundred dollars per share was made in 1825. They have been regularly continued, with few exceptions, averaging something over twelve per cent. per annum, to the present time.

The business of printing calicoes was wholly new in this country. It is true that after it was known that this concern was going into operation for that purpose, two other companies were got up,— one at Dover, N. H., the other at Taunton, Mass., in both of which goods were probably printed before they were by the Merrimack Company. The bringing of the business of printing to any degree of perfection was a matter of difficulty and time. Mr. Allan Pollock thought himself competent to manage it, and was employed for some time. Through the good offices of Mr. Timothy Wiggin, Mr. John D. Prince, of Manchester, was induced to come out, with his family, in

1826, to take charge of the concern, and continued in the service of the Company until 1855. He was then relieved, by a younger man, from the more active duties. On account of his long services, and the great skill and success with which he had conducted that department, he was by the Directors granted an annuity of two thousand dollars per annum, for life.

The then recent improvements in printing were of the highest importance. The old process of printing by blocks of wood was in a great measure superseded by the cylinder. The introduction of machines, carrying one or more cylinders, each distributing a different color, was in printing what the invention of Arkwright was in spinning, the source of immense fortunes. Amongst those who availed themselves of it, one of the earliest was the father of the late Sir Robert Peel, who acquired enormous wealth as a printer. It is related of him, that on his London bankers hinting to him that he was using his credit too freely, he quieted their scruples by revealing to them his secret, that he was coining a guinea on every piece of calico which he printed.

The engraving of these cylinders was a most important part of the process, and Mr. Boott made one voyage to England solely for the purpose of engaging engravers. The art was then kept a very close mystery, and all exportation of machinery was prohibited. Dr. Samuel L. Dana was employed as chemist, and through the superior skill and talent of Messrs. Boott,

Prince and Dana, the Company was brought to the highest degree of success.

In 1828 an arrangement was made by which Mr. J. W. Paige came into the selling agency on the retirement of Mr. Ward from the firm; and it is not too much to say, that to his skill and good judgment the Company is greatly indebted for its success. This office combined with it the preparation of the patterns under a regular designer, and carried with it a commission of $1\frac{1}{4}$ per cent.

Mr. Warren Colburn was for several years superintendent of the mills, and was succeeded by Mr. John Clark, who held the office until 1848, to the great satisfaction of the Directors.

The first printing cloths were made 30 inches wide in the grey, giving them when printed a width of 27 inches, being about two inches above the average of British prints. None other than fast colors were used, whilst a superior durability from the throstle over mule spinning, combined to give them a higher character than attached to any other goods. In the mean time, Mr. Moody was transferred from Waltham to this place, having charge of the manufacture of machinery in the building erected for that purpose. Mr. Worthen had been employed at an early day. He was a man of superior mechanical genius, and his death, in 1824, was deeply regretted.

At the annual meeting at Chelmsford, May 21, 1823, the Directors were authorised to petition for an increase of capital to 1,200,000 dollars, and on the 19th of October, 1824, a new subscription of six hundred shares was voted, and a committee appointed to consider the expediency of organizing the Canal Company, by selling them all the land and water power not required by the Merrimack Manufacturing Company. This committee reported on the 28th February, 1825, in favor of the measure, which was adopted; and at the same time a subscription was opened, by which twelve hundred shares in the Locks and Canals were allotted to the holders of that number of shares in the Merrimack Company, share for share.

The Locks and Canals were thus the owners of all the land and water power in Lowell. They made the necessary new canals to bring it into use. The second mill built at Waltham contained 3584 spindles, spinning No. 14 yarn, with all the apparatus necessary to convert cotton into cloth. This was taken as the standard for what was called a mill power, or the right to draw twenty-five cubic feet per second, on a fall of thirty feet, equal, according to Mr. Francis, to about sixty horse powers, for which the price fixed on was four dollars a spindle, or 14,336 dollars for a mill power and as much land as was proper for the establishment. Of this, 5000 dollars were to remain subject to an annual rent of 300 dollars.

The first sale was to the Hamilton Manufacturing Company, in 1825, with a capital of 600,000 dollars, afterwards increased to 1,200,000. This Company secured the services of Mr. Samuel Batchelder, of New Ipswich, who had shown much skill in manufacturing industry. Under his management the power loom was applied to the weaving of twilled and fancy goods, with great success. The article of cotton drills, since become so important a commodity in our foreign trade, was first made in this establishment. The Appleton Company and the Lowell Company followed, in 1828. In 1829 a violent commercial revulsion took place both in Europe and this country. It was especially felt by the cotton manufacturers in England, and several establishments in this country operating with insufficient capital, were prostrated. The Merrimack Manufacturing Company made no dividend that year. During this period of depression, Messrs. Amos and Abbot Lawrence were induced, by some tempting reduction in the terms made by the Proprietors of the Locks and Canals, to enter largely into the business; the consequence of which was the establishment of the Suffolk, Tremont and Lawrence Companies, in 1830. The Boott followed in 1835, the Massachusetts in 1839. These Companies involve capital amounting to twelve millions of dollars. They are all joint stock companies, with a treasurer as the responsible agent, and a superintendent or manager of the mills. The principle on which these corporations have been established, has always been, the filling of these important offices with men of the highest character and talent which could be obtained. It has been thought, and has been found to be, the best economy, to pay such salaries as will command the entire services of such men. The Directors properly consist of stockholders most largely interested in the management of their own property. They receive nothing for their services. A very important part also depends on the selling agents, who should be well acquainted with the principles of trade. The success of the establishments at Lowell, may be fairly quoted in favor of the system pursued. It is true that during the present revulsion, the most severe within the memory of the oldest merchant, there is a disposition to attribute the depression of the cotton manufacture to the construction of these companies. It is always easy in such a time to find some new ground of cavil. Corporations, like individuals, will succeed or fail, as they are directed by skill and intelligence, or without them.

The chief trouble, in fact, is with those concerns which have attempted to get on with inadequate capital. The Lowell companies were all originally established on the principle that not more than two thirds of the capital should be invested in fixtures and machinery, leaving one third free to carry on the business. In some few instances this principle has been disadvantageously encroached upon, by increasing the original machinery without a proportional increase of capital. One thing is certain, manufactures cannot be carried on to any great extent in this country in any other manner than by joint stock companies. A large capital is necessary to success. Individuals possessing sufficient capital will not give themselves up to this pursuit. It is contrary to the genius of the country.

There are two leading causes for the depression during the last few years. In consequence of the great profits in the years 1844, 5 and 6, both in England and this country, the manufacture was extended beyond the wants of the country; and the disturbances in China have interfered materially with our increasing trade to that region.

It is also evident that the tariff of 1846 has had a most injurious effect upon the cotton manufacture. This is shown most conclusively by the increased exports from England to this country, as stated from official documents in "Burns' Commercial Glance," a paper published in Manchester, under the patronage of the Manchester Chamber of Commerce. It gives the following as the exports of cotton goods to the United States, in millions of yards, for the years

	1844	1845	1846	1854	1855	1856
Plain Calicoes, -	10	12	10	70	81	85
Printed and dyed do.	12	13	13½	78	81	97

Showing an increase, since the passage of the tariff of 1846, of over 600 per cent., without including a large amount from the Clyde. The entire repeal of the minimum has been ruinous to attempts to carry the manufacture into the higher branches, especially in fancy goods. A continued duty of 3 or even 2 cents the square yard, would have saved the manufacturer from heavy losses.

It is a singular circumstance, that whilst in 1816 William Lowndes and John C. Calhoun saw clearly the benefit which the cotton planting States would derive from the introduction of the manufacture into the country, the cotton planters themselves have ever been the most deadly enemies of the manufacture which has done so much for the increase of the consumption of cotton.

It was the Americans who first introduced the manufacture of heavy goods by the application of the least amount of labor to the greatest quantity of raw material, thus producing a description of goods cheaper to the consumer than any heretofore existing. This system the English have been obliged to follow, and have even adopted our name of domestics, whilst they have the advantage of using the cheaper cotton of India, which the Americans have not yet done, but which they will surely find themselves compelled to do.

In 1818, Mr. Calhoun visited the establishment at Waltham, with the apparent satisfaction of having himself contributed to its success. It is lamentable to think that in 1832, under the alluring vision of a separate Southern confederacy, he should have become the active enemy of the manufacture which was doing so much for the interest of the planters, and that the influence of his name has continued to keep them in that error.

In November, 1824, it was voted to petition the Legislature to set off a part of Chelmsford as a separate township. The town of Lowell was incorporated in 1826. It was a matter of some difficulty to fix upon a name for it. I met Mr. Boott one day, when he said to me that the committee of the Legislature were ready to report the bill. It only remained to fill the blank with the name. He said he considered the question narrowed down to two, Lowell or Derby. I said to him, "then Lowell by all means," and Lowell it was.

There was a particular propriety in giving it that name, not only from Mr. Francis C. Lowell, who established the system which gave birth to the place, but also from the interest taken by the family. His son, of the same name, was for some time Treasurer of the Merrimack Company. Mr. John A. Lowell, his nephew, succeeded Mr. Jackson as Treasurer of the Waltham Company, and was for many years Treasurer of the Boott and Massachusetts mills; was largely interested, and a Director in several other Companies. There is no man whose beneficial influence in establishing salutary regulations in relation to this manufacture was exceeded by that of Mr. John A. Lowell. The name of Derby was suggested by Mr. Boott, probably, from his family associations with that place, it being also in the immediate vicinity of one of the earliest seats of the cotton manufacture.

In 1836, the municipal government of Lowell was changed to that of a city.

The capital of the Merrimack Company was further increased 300,000 dollars, in 1828; 500,000 in 1837, and 500,000 in 1849; making the present amount of 2,500,000 dollars.

The death of Mr. Boott, in 1837, was a severe loss

to Lowell. He was a high toned gentleman, of good education. He had acquired the elements of engineering at a government establishment in England, was a man of great energy and intelligence, and by his ingenuous and manly deportment gained the confidence of all with whom he came in contact. His place as Treasurer of the Merrimack Company, was supplied for a short time by Mr. Francis C. Lowell, and then by Mr. Ebenezer Chadwick, the success of whose administration gave the best evidence of his fitness for the office. He died in 1854, and was succeeded by Mr. Francis B. Crowninshield, the present incumbent.

The prices of Merrimack prints have varied as follows:—

The average price per yard in 1825 was	23,07 cents.
" " " " " " 1830 "	16,36 "
" " " " " " 1835 "	16,04 "
" " " " " " 1840 "	12,09 "
" " " " " " 1845 "	10,90 "
" " " " " " 1850 "	9,24 "
" " " " " " 1855 "	9,15 "

Population of Lowell in 1830, was	6,477
" " " " 1840, "	20,981
" " " " 1850, "	32,620
" " " " 1855, "	37,553

The building of machinery was continued by the Proprietors of the Locks and Canals until 1845, when the machine shop and boarding houses appurtenant were sold to a separate corporation; at which time the remaining lands were sold at auction, and the proceeds divided among the stockholders.

In 1846 an improvement of great importance was made by the Locks and Canals Company. It was found that the current of the original canal was so great under the increased use of the water, as materially to diminish its effective power. It was therefore determined to create the present grand canal along the bank of the river, a work which does the greatest honor to the engineer, J. B. Francis. Its cost was over 500.000 dollars, which hardly exceeded his estimate.

A further important measure was the purchase of the outlet of lake Winnipisseogee, and of the rights necessary to control it. A change was also made in the tenure of the water power, by which the different corporations became joint owners of it as proprietors instead of partial lessees, as heretofore.

The original water wheels were made upon the principle recommended by Smeaton, the hydraulic engineer, supposed, when constructed in the most perfect manner, to give the greatest possible power of the weight of water upon the wheel, with the least possible loss or waste in receiving or discharging it. When constructed in the best manner, however, they were not estimated to realize more than 75 per cent. of the actual power of the water expended.

These have been superseded by the Turbine wheel, a French invention, greatly improved by Uriah A. Boyden, which acts on a vertical shaft through discharging tubes, on the principle of reaction, with no loss from back water other than the loss of head. These have been fully described in an elaborate work by James B. Francis, entitled "Lowell Hydraulic Experiments," showing that they have been found capable of realizing 88 per cent. of the power expended. He estimates the average result at 75 against 60, which he considers the average of the best water wheels.

As the old wheels in Lowell have decayed, they have been replaced by Turbines, until very few of the old ones remain. The whole power used by the mills in Lowell being 139 mill powers, is estimated by Mr. Francis as about equal to 9000 horse powers.

The Boston and Lowell Rail-Road was among the very first established in the United States. So early as 1830 a committee was appointed on the subject, and a bonus of 100,000 dollars was voted by the Locks and Canals Company, payable on its completion. A subscription was obtained, and Mr. Jackson undertook to carry it into effect. His usual energy and enterprise were shown in its completion, with a double track, on a scale of solidity and permanence which has seldom been followed. It was opened for travel in June, 1835, earlier than any other rail-road in Massachusetts, for its entire length, and with the exception of the Camden and Amboy, to Bordentown, in the United States.

www.ingramcontent.com/pod-product-compliance
Lightning Source LLC
LaVergne TN
LVHW011122110826
845150LV00008B/2226

9781418195342